GET GREEN!

Anne Marie Todd

www.heinemann.co.uk/library

Visit our website to find out more information about **Heinemann Library** books.

To order:

☎ Phone 44 (0) 1865 888066

▤ Send a fax to 44 (0) 1865 314091

▢ Visit the Heinemann Bookshop at www.heinemann.co.uk/library to browse our catalogue and order online.

Heinemann Library is an imprint of Pearson Education Limited, a company incorporated in England and Wales having its registered office at Edinburgh Gate, Harlow, Essex, CM20 2JE – Registered company number: 00872828

"Heinemann" is a registered trademark of Pearson Education Limited.

Text © Pearson Education Limited 2009
First published in hardback in 2009
The moral rights of the proprietor have been asserted.

Edited by Pollyanna Poulter
Designed by Philippa Jenkins and Hart MacLeod
Original illustrations © Pearson Education Limited
    by Clare Elsom and Gary Slater
Picture research by Elizabeth Alexander and
    Maria Joannou
Production by Alison Parsons
Originated by Modern Age Repro House Ltd.
Printed and bound in China by South China
    Printing Company Ltd.

ISBN 978 0 431112 39 8 (hardback)
13 12 11 10 09
10 9 8 7 6 5 4 3 2 1

British Library Cataloguing-in-Publication Data
Todd, Anne Marie
Get green! - (Life skills)
1. Conservation of natural resources - Juvenile literature
I. Title
333.7'2
A full catalogue record for this book is available from the British Library.

Acknowledgements
We would like to thank the following for permission to reproduce photographs: © Alamy Images: pp. **11** (Tim Hill), **47** (Jeff Greenberg); © Corbis: pp. **19** (Klaus Hackenberg/Zefa), **36** (Szilard Koszticsak/EPA), **43** (Roger Ressmeyer); © The Fairtrade Foundation: p. **16 left**; © Getty Images: pp. **6** (Guang Niu), **15** (Riser/Sonya Farrell), **31** (Photolibrary/Ron Evans); © Istockphoto: p. **22** (Andrzej Tokarski); © NASA: p. **4**; © PA Photos: p. **49** (AP/Dima Gavrysh); © Permission to use the Fair Trade Certified™ logo was granted by TransFair USA: p. **16 right**; © Photolibrary: pp. **12** (Bill Boch), **21** (Imagestate), **24** (Beuthan Beuthan), **38** (Randy Faris); © Rex Features: pp. **33** (Alisdair Macdonald), **35** (Stewart Cook), **45**; © Science Photo Library: pp. **27** (Robert Brook), **40** (Martin Bond).

Cover photograph of recycle bin with wheat grass reproduced with permission of © Punchstock (Digital Vision).

We would like to thank Michael Mastrandrea for his invaluable help in the preparation of this book.

Every effort has been made to contact copyright holders of material reproduced in this book. Any omissions will be rectified in subsequent printings if notice is given to the Publishers.

Contents

Some words are printed in bold, **like this**. You can find out
what they mean by looking in the glossary.

OUR GLOBAL ENVIRONMENT

How would you feel if your friends came over and dumped rubbish all over your house, giving no thought to the results of their actions? Well, in many ways, that's how humans have been treating our home – planet Earth.

←

The awe-inspiring beauty of Earth from space is a reminder that humans are bound together on this planet.

LOOKING AFTER OUR HOME

People are used to thinking of themselves as part of a local community. But they need to realise they are also part of the global community. The problems Earth faces are so large and complex that they can seem daunting at times. In order to combat these problems, it is useful to think of Earth as our home. Most people know how important it is to take care of their home and keep it clean so they don't destroy it. Well, Earth is our home as well, and it's the only one we have.

Earth is a complex **ecosystem**, in which plants and animals depend on one another – and humans are part of that system. Earth supports living organisms by providing air, water, and food.

DID YOU KNOW?

The **Gaia hypothesis** is a theory by Dr. James Lovelock. Named after the ancient Greek goddess of Earth, the Gaia hypothesis states that Earth is a complex, interacting system that functions like a single organism. Lovelock argues that life on Earth is possible because of the working balance of Earth's environment. His hypothesis aims to show that because all life is connected in the ecosystem, all the living things on Earth directly influence its temperature and composition.

Humans rely on Earth's life-support system, too. We need clean water to drink and to bathe ourselves, fertile land to produce food, and forests for wood to make paper and furniture. Through careless activity, however, we have depleted Earth's **natural resources** and damaged the health of the environment.

Today, Earth is in crisis. Humans have had a profound effect on the environment. Through centuries of activity – from building and manufacturing to car and air travel – we have used up valuable resources and caused harmful pollution. Because past generations weren't aware of the effects of their actions on the planet, they got into some bad habits. Today we need to act fast to do something about it!

Earth is a global ecosystem and all life on it is interconnected. Our ecosystem acts as a life support for plants and animals. Rain and sunlight carry nutrients and energy to plants and trees, which support human and animal life.

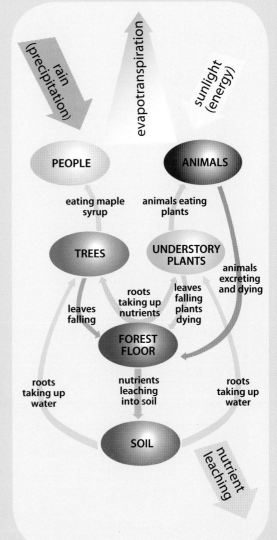

rain (precipitation)

evapotranspiration

sunlight (energy)

PEOPLE

ANIMALS

eating maple syrup

animals eating plants

TREES

UNDERSTORY PLANTS

animals excreting and dying

roots taking up nutrients

leaves falling plants dying

leaves falling

FOREST FLOOR

roots taking up water

nutrients leaching into soil

roots taking up water

SOIL

nutrient leaching

HUMAN RESPONSIBILITY

Our actions have an impact on the health of the planet, so everyone has a responsibility to behave in ways that reduce harm to Earth. By adopting a **sustainable** lifestyle, we can support our own needs while preserving Earth for later generations.

The good news is, each person's actions can make a difference. A person's **ecological footprint**, or environmental impact, is measured by the area of land required to support that person. By making smart choices about how you consume Earth's resources, you can reduce your ecological footprint.

In this book, you will discover many ways you can get green, or become more environmentally responsible. Green awareness involves making informed choices that reduce your ecological footprint. Added together, several smart choices can go a long way toward lessening your impact on Earth.

As just one person on this vast planet, it may feel like what you do every day doesn't matter. But it most certainly does! Your actions can also influence the actions of others. If you and your family – and all your friends and their families – pitched in and adopted a green lifestyle, it would make a huge difference.

Gridlock is a common sight in many cities. Using other ways to get to work and school reduces the number of cars on the road, and can significantly reduce air pollution.

Best of all, being green doesn't just help the planet – it also helps humans. For example, reducing air pollution helps reduce breathing problems that are common in many crowded cities. And reducing water pollution gives more people around the world access to clean drinking water.

The important thing to remember is that you can make a difference every day!

Climate change

Climate change, or **global warming**, is caused by the emission of greenhouse gases, such as carbon dioxide (CO_2), produced by burning **fossil fuels**, such as coal, oil, and gasoline. Other greenhouse gases include: nitrogen oxide, produced by cars and coal-burning power plants used to generate electricity; methane, produced by rotting waste in landfills; and chlorofluorocarbons (CFCs), produced by manufacturing plastic.

While there are natural sources of greenhouse gases, scientists have shown that recent climate change is the result of human-made greenhouse gases. The IPCC (Intergovernmental Panel on Climate Change) predicts that Earth will warm to between 1.1°C (34°F) and 6.4°C (44°F) by the end of this century.

Getting it Right

Being green means making smart choices about:

- The food you eat and where it comes from,
- How you use energy (electricity, fuel, petrol),
- How you use water,
- What you wear,
- How you dispose of your rubbish,
- How you travel from one place to another.

The actual rise in temperature depends on the level of future emissions and how Earth's ecosystems respond to them.

To understand how this warming could affect the planet, consider that a cooling to 6°C (43°F) of Earth's average temperature is the difference between our current climate and an ice age. So imagine how hot Earth will be if it gets warmer by the same amount!

Getting it Wrong

Though power plants are a major source of greenhouse gases, individuals also contribute to climate change. Every time you go somewhere by car, or buy bottled water, you're creating greenhouse gas emissions. The average home contributes as much to climate change per year as the average car!

Greenhouse gases, such as carbon dioxide, trap energy from the Sun in the Earth's atmosphere and warm our world. What are some of the ways that you contribute to greenhouse gas emissions?

Upsetting the balance

As the Gaia hypothesis (see page 5) noted, Earth's ecosystem relies on a delicate balance of conditions. Severe changes in Earth's climate will upset the balance essential to supporting life.

DID YOU KNOW?

The 2003 heat wave in Europe that killed tens of thousands of people was partly a result of global warming. In its latest report, the United Nations warned that climate change will have catastrophic results for human populations in many parts of the world.

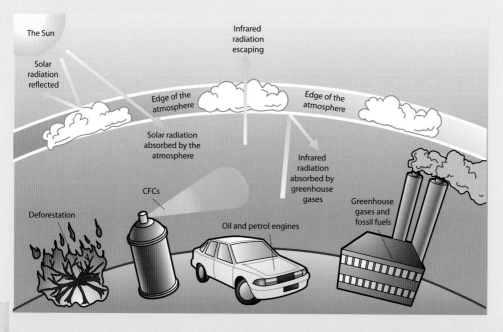

The Sun

Solar radiation reflected

Infrared radiation escaping

Edge of the atmosphere

Edge of the atmosphere

Solar radiation absorbed by the atmosphere

Infrared radiation absorbed by greenhouse gases

CFCs

Greenhouse gases and fossil fuels

Deforestation

Oil and petrol engines

As the climate warms, melting glaciers will make sea levels rise. Widespread flooding could destroy coastal cities and towns. In the United States, New York City and large parts of Florida could be entirely underwater!

Warmer temperatures will mean less rain and frequent and intense droughts. This will make farming difficult in many parts of the world and some places uninhabitable. Heat-related health problems will also occur across the world.

Getting it Right

In 1988, the United Nations set up a group of 2,500 researchers from over 130 nations to advise governments on the challenges of climate change. In 2007, this group – the Intergovernmental Panel on Climate Change (IPCC) – along with former U.S. Vice President Al Gore, won the Nobel Peace Prize for their efforts to raise public awareness of climate change. The prize committee said Gore had done the most to inform the world about climate change. So individual action can make a difference!

QUIZ

HOW GREEN ARE YOU?

1) When you travel somewhere, do you mostly:
   a) walk or bike?
   b) take public transport?
   c) drive?

2) How often do you and your family turn off lights and appliances when you have finished using them?
   a) Always.
   b) Sometimes.
   c) Never.

3) How often does your family recycle or compost waste?
   a) Always.
   b) Sometimes.
   c) Never.

4) How often does your family buy organic, local, or minimally processed food?
   a) Always.
   b) Sometimes.
   c) Never.

5) How many of your clothes or toys are secondhand?
   a) Many.
   b) Some.
   c) Few or none.

Check page 50 to see how green you are.

Eating The Planet

When you eat a meal, how often do you think about what it's made of and where it came from? It's time to think more carefully about what you're consuming.

Healthy Choices

We make choices about food all the time. Most people understand that what we choose to eat affects our health. But people often fail to realise that what we eat also affects the environment. In the school cafeteria, the supermarket, or at home, what you decide to put in your mouth has a direct impact on Earth's resources.

Sustainable agriculture

For centuries, small farmers supplied food to feed their local community. In the early 1900s, however, to feed Earth's growing population, this old model of food production evolved into **industrial agriculture**. This system produces enormous quantities of food on large plots of land. Today, large-scale industrial farms produce much of the world's food. It has serious drawbacks. One is that it requires an enormous amount of energy. While estimates vary, a 2005 study claims that, taking into account water needed to irrigate crops for feed, nearly half of all water in the United States is used to raise livestock. Producing just one kilogram of beef takes an average of 10 kg of grain and 680 litres of water!

Part of going green means choosing sustainable methods of food production. This involves cutting down the number of **food miles** in your diet. Food miles represent the distance it travels from its origin to the consumer – from the farm to the table.

Have you ever had strawberries during the winter? Many of us enjoy out-of-season produce. But those strawberries probably had to travel hundreds, if not thousands, of miles to your table, from another country or continent. Shipping food across the world in vehicles wastes resources and releases harmful greenhouse gases.

Getting it Right

Natural, unprocessed food doesn't contain unhealthy chemical additives or artificial flavours. It saves resources and is better for both you and the environment than processed food.

RECIPE

Fresh tomato sauce is tastier and healthier than processed varieties. It saves on waste packaging and is simple to make.

Ingredients:
Selection of fresh tomatoes, chopped
Handful of fresh basil leaves
Clove of fresh garlic, crushed
Drizzle of olive oil
Pinch of sea salt and black pepper

What to do:
Heat the oil in a pan. Carefully add the tomatoes and garlic. Tear in the basil leaves. Add the salt and pepper. Stir and simmer for 5-10 minutes.

How to use:
Great base for pasta dishes, pizzas, and soups.

Taste tips:
Try a mixture of different tomatoes. Some taste sweeter or stronger than others. If your sauce tastes bitter, try stirring in a little sugar and lemon juice.

Try this:
Grow tomatoes, basil, and garlic at home!

Natural food is better food

Another problem with industrial agriculture is that many of these crops are processed, prepared, or packaged in some way. Processed food uses more energy than food in its natural state. For example, you could buy tomato sauce in a can (processed food) or you could make it from scratch. Raw ingredients, such as tomatoes and herbs, require some energy to grow on the farm. But canned sauce uses up lots more energy – first the raw ingredients are grown, then shipped to a plant, and finally they have to be processed and packaged.

DID YOU KNOW?

A 2005 UK government report found the environmental, social, and economic costs of food transport are about £9 billion ($18 billion) each year. The average vegetable travels 2,092 km (1,300 miles) before arriving at your table! Shipping contributes to carbon emissions. Growing out of season requires large-scale heating and watering systems. All this takes a toll on the environment.

CHOOSING A GREEN DIET

Many factors go into the decision to eat certain foods – you can choose foods that taste good or are nutritious or both. You can also choose foods with a low environmental impact. Fortunately, most people eat about three meals a day, so there are plenty of opportunities to make environmentally friendly choices in your diet!

Buy organic

Organic farming is a way of growing crops without the use of pesticides or synthetic fertilisers. This method has less impact on the environment than large-scale industrial farming. Instead of using pesticides and other toxic chemicals, organic farmers use alternative methods, such as row covers and insect traps, to protect plants from harmful pests. They also employ techniques, such as crop rotation, which involves planting a different crop in a specific area each season to replenish the nutrients in the soil. Organic farming also uses much less water than conventional farming. If your local supermarket doesn't carry organic products, ask them to start stocking options for organic shoppers like you!

DID YOU KNOW?

Buying local food significantly reduces your food miles. Buying vegetables, meat, and dairy products produced by small farmers who sell their goods at a local market is much better for the environment than buying food produced far away and shipped to you. Buying local reduces the amount of energy it takes to make your food.

A local grocer's shop or farmer's market will often stock local and organic produce. Buying these could reduce your ecological footprint!

What's in your family's refrigerator? Check out your freezer, too! Use this list to help make green food choices easy for your family. For each item, ask the following questions:

- Where was it grown or produced? Check the label, sticker, or shop sign.

- How was it grown/produced? Mass-produced or local?

- How many miles did it travel? Imported or homegrown?

- Has it been processed?

- How is it packaged? Does it have an unnecessary amount of packaging?

- Is it organic or **fair trade**?

Eat less processed and packaged food

Food packaging accounts for a third of the contents of the average rubbish bin! It has a high environmental cost. Plastics are produced from **fossil fuels** and their production emits toxic chemicals into the air, water, and soil. Buying food with as little packaging as possible, and composting any biodegradable waste, reduces energy consumption and pollution. It can also save you money – of the average grocery bill, packaging accounts for as much as 10 percent.

Drink fewer canned or bottled drinks

Those cans, cartons, and bottles that hold your favourite drinks have a big environmental impact. Producing glass bottles and aluminium cans uses a lot of energy. It takes four tons of ore to produce one ton of aluminium. Producing glass from scratch requires about 30 percent more energy than producing it from crushed, used glass. Plus, it takes one million years for a glass bottle to break down in a landfill!

Getting it Right

Stainless steel and other reusable water bottles are cool – you can personalize them with stickers or other decorations that reflect your style! Take a bottle with you wherever you go and fill it up from the tap or a water fountain. Bring your lunch in reusable containers as well. By buying food and drink in bulk, your family can use less packaging and save money at the same time.

MORE WAYS TO EAT GREEN

Whether you are at the supermarket or in the cafeteria line, eating green means considering the environmental cost when you choose food.

Eat vegetarian

Many people around the world are **vegetarian**. They eat a plant-based diet with no meat. Vegetarian diets are low in fat and high in fibre, so can reduce the risk of heart disease and obesity. Eating vegetarian can reduce pollution because vegetables require less energy to produce. Producing meat can consume up to eight times as much fossil fuel energy as growing vegetables, because of the energy needed to feed livestock. Raising livestock contributes to **agricultural runoff** and water pollution.

Getting it Right

If you decide to eat vegetarian, be sure to eat a healthy, balanced diet with plenty of protein, iron, and calcium. Talk to your parents or a teacher about good sources of these nutrients if you decide to eat vegetarian. If you don't want to cut out meat entirely, eating vegetarian even a few times a week can provide health benefits and reduce your impact on Earth!

TIP

Ask for advice at your local garden centre. They may be able to tell you what nutrients you will need to add to your soil so your plants grow better. They may also be able to tell you what kind of soil it is (clay, sand, light, heavy) and which plants are best suited to growing in it.

Grow your own food

Planting and harvesting produce from your own garden is rewarding and fun. You can grow your favourite fruits and vegetables from seeds or starter plants found at your local garden centre or supermarket. As a gardener, you will be building and maintaining an ecosystem.

To get started, select part of your garden to serve as a vegetable plot. You will need to prepare and till the soil to make sure it is healthy enough to support plant life.

After planting, the fun starts!

Throughout the growing season, you must tend to your garden. Remove weeds and water your crops to keep them growing. At harvest time, you can enjoy cooking a meal from your very own garden!

↑ *Many kids and young adults around the world are getting into gardening! The Edible Schoolyard in Berkeley, California, USA, is a one-acre organic garden and kitchen classroom. There, 950 students learn how to grow, tend harvest, and prepare healthy seasonal fruit and vegetables.*

DID YOU KNOW?

Even if you don't have a garden, you can still grow your own food. Tomatoes, courgettes, and lettuce grow well in containers with good drainage and access to sunshine. Though there are many different types of containers available, you needn't go out and buy special ones. Poke a few holes in the bottom of an old bucket or basin and you have a recycled container for planting! You can also grow herbs, such as basil, mint, and rosemary, indoors as they require very little space. Alternatively, check out local allotments or find a community garden and share a plot of land with your neighbours.

Supporting green farming

One harmful industrial farming practice is the use of **pesticides** to reduce pest damage to crops. Pesticides work by destroying the life cycle of pests. Large agricultural companies use pesticides to increase their crop yield – and, therefore, increase their profits.

Today nearly half of the world's agricultural land is depleted (the nutrients in it are used up). This means it will be more difficult, if not impossible, to grow crops there in the future.

Studies show that expanding industrial food production is likely to do serious environmental harm as well. For one thing, the practice of monoculture – planting one crop over a large area – destroys the **biodiversity** of the land. For another, it causes agricultural runoff, or pollution that seeps into lakes, streams, and groundwater.

Getting it Right

Because organic farming does not use pesticides, eating organic is a better choice for the environment. It is also a healthier choice for your body. Pesticides may be bad for the soil, but they're even worse for animals and humans!

FAIRTRADE (left) and TransFair (right) marks are used on Fairtrade licenced products in the UK, US, and Canada.

What is fair trade?

Fair trade practices protect the workers and communities involved in food production. They ensure workers are paid fairly and products are made in a way that does not harm them or their community. In the 1980s, an independent organization began to certify products made under these conditions. The first international Fairtrade label was established in 2002. Today, sales of Fairtrade certified goods are growing rapidly.

TIP

When you see a Fairtrade label like those above, you know the farmers or growers earned a fair price for their products.

DID YOU KNOW?

In 1962 an American biologist named Rachel Carson wrote a book called *Silent Spring* that described a chilling future without birds. Carson's research showed that the uncontrolled use of toxic pesticides was polluting the soil and groundwater, causing sickness in humans and killing many animals, especially birds. Her book led to the banning of the dangerous pesticide DDT in the United States in 1972. It also helped spark the environmental movement.

Slow food

The Slow Food movement was founded in Italy in 1986. Its philosophy is that food should taste good and be produced in a clean way that does not harm the environment. It also believes that food producers should be paid fairly for their work. Today, more than 80,000 people worldwide are involved in the movement. Slow Food supporters are reacting against today's fast-food culture of meals on the go. They urge people to enjoy food slowly and to take pleasure in a good meal made from fresh, locally-grown ingredients.

QUIZ

WHAT'S YOUR FOOD FOOTPRINT?

1) How often do you eat meat products (such as beef, pork, chicken, and fish)?
   a) Never or rarely (vegan or vegetarian).
   b) Sometimes (meat once or twice a week).
   c) Very often (meat in almost every meal).

2) How much of the food you eat is processed, packaged, and not locally grown (from more than 200 miles away)?
   a) Very little (most of your food is grown locally and is unprocessed).
   b) Less than half.
   c) All of the food you eat is imported, processed, or packaged.

3) How much food do you throw away?
   a) Almost none (you buy in bulk and save food in reusable containers).
   b) Less than half (you finish most food on your plate or in your refrigerator).
   c) Nearly all of the food in your refrigerator or cabinet spoils before it is eaten.

Check page 50 to see how your food footprint measures up.

Using Energy

How often do you remember to switch off the lights when you leave a room? Always? Sometimes? Never? In the same way that the planet provides us with food to fuel our bodies, it also provides us with energy to power our activities. When we turn on a light, take a hot shower, or do homework on a computer, we are consuming energy. Energy use is responsible for a big part of our ecological footprint. This is because creating energy uses up Earth's natural resources.

Nonrenewable Energy

One of the most common forms of energy is electricity. Today much of the world's electrical power comes from **nonrenewable energy** sources. Nonrenewable energy sources cannot be replenished. Once we run out of them, we run out for good!

The most common nonrenewable energy sources are coal, oil, and natural gas. About 86 percent of the world's energy comes from burning fossil fuels. This is a major factor that contributes to global warming.

Burning fossil fuels to make electricity also causes air pollution. This leads to breathing problems, such as asthma, in humans and harms plant life. Asthma rates have gone up 50 percent in the last 10 years, as air pollution has increased. The highest asthma rates in the world amongst children can be found in Scotland. And in the United States alone, 6 million children now have asthma.

• CHECKLIST •

Conduct an energy audit of your house. Make a list of all the appliances in your home. Use it to help you apply the energy-saving tips on the next few pages in your own home! For each appliance, ask yourself the following questions:

- How many times a day do I use it?

- Does it have a standby or low-power mode?

- Is it normally left on after each use?

- Does it have a timer or motion-sensor?

Skyscrapers use electricity when people aren't in them. With lights on, they disorientate night-migrating birds during autumn and spring. So some cities dim the lights at these times.

Average personal CO_2 emissions in a developed country			
Heating house	**Heating water and cooking**	**Lighting and appliances**	**Total individual emissions**
1.2 tonnes (1.33 US tons	0.4 tonnes (0.5 US tons)	0.7 tonnes (0.8 US tons)	2.3 tonnes (2.63 US tons)

TIPS FOR CONSERVING ENERGY

There are many ways to reduce energy use around the house and lessen your ecological footprint. Plus, reducing energy use will help your household cut costs! Below are a few easy ways to **conserve** energy at home. Remember to discuss these tips with a parent or guardian before putting them into action!

G Turn off lights

Turning off lights when you leave a room can make a big difference in your electricity use. You might want to put up sticky notes around the house to remind yourself and your family until it becomes a habit.

TIP

For any lights that stay on for long periods of time, such as outdoor lights, your family can install a timer to turn them on and off automatically. This can help reduce the amount of time they are on, and the amount of energy they use!

Getting it Right

You can also improve how energy efficient your home is by sealing any holes or gaps where drafts get through. This will help keep your home warmer during winter and cooler during summer. Find out where the holes are in your house and help your parents seal them with filler or draught excluders. Popular places where cold drafts can get in and warm air can escape are around windowpanes and doorframes. Closing curtains and blinds after dark can also help insulate your home from the cold.

G Be smart about heating and cooling

During the winter, ask someone at home to set your thermostat lower. This will keep your house at a slightly cooler temperature. You can always put a jumper on to stay warm. Remember to turn down the heat if you and your family are gone during the day. If you go on holiday, turn off the heat.

During the summer, keep your thermostat set higher so you use less air conditioning. Use fans instead – they use less energy. Of course, if your home doesn't have air conditioning, you're already doing your part for the environment! To stay cool, wear loose, breathable clothing and drink plenty of cool water. Keeping curtains and blinds closed on sunny summer days can also help keep it cooler inside.

G   Use less hot water

It takes a lot of energy to heat water. Ask someone at home to turn down the water heater thermostat to 49°C (120°F) – this can save energy and money! Use cold water to wash your hands and your clothes. Only put the

Air drying can save substantial amounts of electricity. Install a clothesline so you can help make laundry earth-friendly!

amount of water you need in kettles and pans so less energy is used to heat it.

Washing your clothes in cold water can also save energy. Dryers use a lot of electricity, so use the shortest or coolest cycle possible. Or, better yet, ask someone to install a clothesline and hang up your clothes to air dry.

DID YOU KNOW?

Using your dryer for just one hour less a week could cut your family's annual emissions by 0.7 tonnes (0.8 US tons). Not using it at all could increase that energy saving!

MORE ENERGY SAVING TIPS

Some energy saving tips seem obvious but can be easily overlooked. Little changes can make a huge difference.

(G) Turn off appliances when not in use

Many appliances continue to use energy even when they are turned off. Turning off or unplugging appliances when you're not using them will cut down on wasted energy. Use energy-saving settings on dishwashers, washing machines, and dryers. When using the dishwasher, do not use the drying feature – it increases energy consumption. And keep the refrigerator cool by closing the door right away after you get what you need.

(G) Use energy-efficient bulbs

Incandescent bulbs are inefficient – they give off 90 percent of their energy as heat, not light. **Compact fluorescent bulbs** use 75 percent less energy and last 10 times longer. In a fluorescent light bulb, an electrical current causes a chemical reaction between the materials in the tube. This creates light more efficiently, minus the heat of an incandescent bulb.

Compact fluorescent bulbs (CFBs) conserve energy. How many light bulbs would you need to replace in your house?

TIP

The next time someone you know is buying a new appliance, such as a refrigerator or washer-dryer, encourage them to buy the most energy-efficient model. This will save them a lot of money and help the environment, too!

Work with your community

Communities can work together to reduce their collective energy consumption.

At home, at school, at work

Look for ways you can reduce your school's energy use. Are lights or computers left on at night? Turning them off instead saves energy and helps your school reduce its monthly costs.

Other members of your community may be wasting energy and not be aware of it. Do any businesses in your town leave their lights on all night? If so, politely ask them to turn off their lights to save energy. You'll be surprised at how much power you have as both an individual and a consumer.

DID YOU KNOW?

Recycling is a great way to reduce your energy consumption. Recycling just 125 aluminium cans saves enough energy to power one home for 24 hours. Recycling one glass bottle saves enough energy to light a 100-watt light bulb for four hours or operate a television for four hours.

Once you have figured out an energy-saving plan for your family, talk to your friends and neighbours about your family's environmental choices. Remember, every household needs to make their own energy decisions. But by sharing your own experiences you can help them understand how easy it is to get green!

Getting it Right

In February 2007, Australia announced a nationwide ban on incandescent bulbs. The ban will take effect in 2010. The policy is expected to reduce greenhouse gas emissions by 800,000 tons by 2012.

RENEWABLE ENERGY

Unlike nonrenewable energy sources that can run out, **renewable energy** sources can be replenished in a short timeframe. The most common examples are wind, water, and sunlight.

How do these renewable methods work?

The energy of moving water forms hydropower. On vast wind farms, rows of large **turbines** turn wind power into energy. Special solar panels and cells, usually installed on the roof or side of a building, use energy from the Sun to generate electricity or heat water. These renewable sources are often called **alternative energy** sources because they present a more sustainable alternative to fossil fuels.

This house has solar panels. The owners get their electricity from an alternative energy source. Installing solar panels can be expensive but are a worthwhile investment and can replace a monthly electricity bill. More and more cities are providing incentives for families to go solar!

Using renewable sources will help conserve Earth's natural resources for future generations. While most of the world's energy still comes from burning fossil fuels, alternative energy sources are cropping up all over the world – and they're becoming cheaper all the time. Many communities already invest in alternative energy.

Energy perks

Some cities even provide incentives, such as tax breaks, to families that use renewable energy. You can encourage your parents or guardians to support new laws that make it easier for homes and businesses to use green energy. Perhaps someday soon all of the world's energy will come from renewable sources!

What you can do at home

Those beautiful strands of lights hung outdoors during the Christmas holidays use a lot of energy. Leaving them on all day and night wastes electricity. If you have Christmas decoration lights, ask a parent or guardian to put them on a timer so they will only be on during the early evening when people are most likely to see and enjoy them.

Getting it Right

Talk to your teachers about starting a project to reduce your school's energy usage. Consider having a class "energy monitor" – whose job is to make sure lights are turned off when no one is using a room. You and your classmates can take turns doing this job!

QUIZ

HOW ENERGY SMART ARE YOU?

1) True or false: appliances that are turned off don't use any electricity.

2) How much longer than an incandescent bulb does a compact fluorescent bulb last?

3) True or false: curtains can reduce energy lost through a window by half.

4) True or false: recycling saves energy.

Check your answers on page 50 to see how energy smart you are.

Water Conservation

Do you leave the water running when you brush your teeth or wash the dishes? Think about the gallons of water you use. Can you think of any ways to reduce it?

Water, water, everywhere

We use lots of water. We use it for drinking, cooking, brushing our teeth, washing our clothes, and much, much more. Global water use has tripled since 1950 and has been increasing faster than the world's population.

Overuse of the water supply has led to water shortages, or droughts, in some areas. This makes life difficult for people, who must severely restrict their water use. Drought affects the entire ecosystem, threatening plant and animal life. When river beds or other water sources dry up, animals must change their migration patterns. As a result, drought can reduce the biodiversity of a region and upset the ecosystem's natural balance.

Getting it Right

Limiting your family's water use is an important step toward conserving this precious resource. Monitor how many litres of water your household uses each day. In a typical home, each member uses nearly 200 litres a day. A running tap uses 6 litres of water per minute! Each time you wash your hands, rinse an apple, or take a shower, think about the cost of your water use.

DID YOU KNOW?

A report by the World Wide Fund for Nature (WWF) in 2001, stated that roughly 1.5 million tons of plastic is used each year to bottle almost 89 billion litres of water. The energy required to make the bottles and transport them to stores contributes to climate change. Many bottles will end up in a landfill where they take millions of years to break down, and release toxic chemicals into the ground. Recycling plastic bottles is a better alternative, but even this uses energy!

Getting it Wrong

Water is a precious resource, but we don't always treat it that way. Human activity has led to two major threats to our water reserves: pollution and overuse. Dumping chemicals and other waste into clean water sources, such as lakes, rivers, and oceans, has led to widespread water pollution. This threatens our supply of clean drinking water, poisons aquatic life, and can make swimming at beaches unsafe.

Plastic bottles and other waste pollute streams and other local waterways. Ask your teacher to help you organise a clean-up in your local town. With your help, local animals and birds will live healthier lives.

TIPS FOR SAVING WATER

Below are many ways to cut down on water use at home. Look in every room of your home and try to come up with some more of your own!

In the living room: When someone in your family doesn't finish a glass of water, don't pour it down the drain. Collect the water in a watering can and use it to water houseplants. Or, if it rains a lot where you live, collect rainwater in a bucket outside to water your indoor and outdoor plants.

Outside: Using a broom rather than a hose to clean driveways, walkways, and steps can save hundreds of litres of water. If you politely explain this to your neighbours, maybe they will take action. You could even offer to sweep their driveway for them!

In the bathroom: Take fewer baths and shorter showers. A three-minute shower uses less than a quarter of the water needed for a bath. When brushing your teeth, don't leave the tap running. Leaving the water on wastes more than 6 litres of water. Just wet and rinse your brush and you will use only half a litre of water each time.

A typical toilet uses 8 to 12 litres per flush. Ask a parent or guardian to help you install a water-displacement device that allows less water to fill the tank.

In the kitchen: Washing dishes by hand uses up to 50 percent more water than an efficient dishwasher. Keeping the tap flowing while washing dishes can use as much as 100 litres of water! Wipe excess fat off cooking utensils before washing them so less water is required to rinse them clean. Use biodegradable detergent (detergent that breaks down quickly and doesn't pollute) to reduce water pollution. Also, never thaw food by running it under the tap – instead, leave it in the refrigerator or on the worksurface to thaw.

Everywhere: Install low-flow water devices indoors and out. These devices can drastically reduce water use throughout the home. A normal tap flows at a rate of six litres per minute. A low-flow faucet head aerates the water (fills it with tiny air bubbles), reducing water flow by up to 50 percent. Installing low-flow heads on showers and taps could save a family of four around 1000 litres of water a month. That's a total of 12,000 litres of water a year!

In the laundry room: The laundry room accounts for 20 percent of household water use. Do full loads, and if you have a small load, only use the amount of water necessary. Also, use biodegradable laundry detergent. Conventional detergents contain chemicals that harm the water supply.

Water audit

Your water bill tells you how many litres of water your household uses in a month. Divide this by 30 to find out how much water you use on an average day. You can also estimate water use in your house by measuring water flow from each fixture:

- Taps and showerheads (indoor and outdoor): run the water into a container for 10 seconds. Measure the water and multiply that number by six. This is the flow rate in litres per minute.
- Toilets: estimate 6 litres per flush. If your toilet is less than 15 years old, estimate 4.5 litres.
- Washing machine: estimate 50 litres per use.
- Dishwasher: estimate 20 litres per use.

Next, estimate how many minutes a day you use each tap. Multiply the water flow for each tap by the number of minutes. Multiply the flow rate for each appliance by the number of times the appliance is used each day.

Add the figures to get your family's daily water use. Divide this by the number of people in your household, and you have your per capita (per person) rate of water usage. The average person's daily water use ranges from 200 to 300 litres a day in Europe and the United States. How do you and your family rate?

DID YOU KNOW?

Many communities reuse grey water. That is water that has been put to household use but doesn't contain contaminants. For example, it can be used to water landscaping.

In the garden

Choose environmentally friendly landscaping. Native plants that can survive on your area's average rainfall are best. Only water when necessary and if there is a drought, stop watering. Mulching the roots helps conserve water. Morning watering will prevent the sun's midday heat from evaporating the water before it soaks into the soil. Ensure you water the roots, not the leaves, and that your sprinkler waters the garden and not the pavement! Install a waterbutt under drainpipes to catch rainwater and use it to water your garden.

Household appliance water use	
Appliance	**Litres consumed per use**
Toilet per flush	6 litres
One bath	80 litres
10-minute shower	50 litres
One washing machine load	50 litres
One dishwasher load	20 litres

Native landscaping can reduce water usage and help support local wildlife. It provides proper nutrients, such as seeds and pollen, that are part of the local ecosystem.

Travelling Green

How often do you travel by car each week? To school and back? To the supermarket? To see friends? Where else? What about air travel? Have you ever travelled by plane to another city?

TRANSPORTATION IMPACTS

Today, it's fairly easy to get in a car or plane and go where you want. But do you ever think about the consequences? Travel habits greatly contribute to our ecological footprint. Car and plane engines run on fossil fuels, so they produce carbon emissions on a very large scale.

Cars and lorries are a major source of carbon emissions. For many, driving is their most polluting daily activity. The United States produces 25 percent of all human-caused, greenhouse gas emissions. Transportation accounts for a third of this. This makes U.S. drivers some of the biggest contributors to air pollution and global warming! One reason is that more than 70 percent of the cars on American roads are more than 10 years old.

Air travel is another contributor to carbon emissions. Many people travel by plane more than once a year. These trips take a toll on the environment. For example, a single trip from London to New York emits nearly three tons of carbon dioxide. Frequent flyers have carbon footprints up to 10 times larger than average.

Many people who fly for business do not have much choice about where or how often they fly. But you have more control over where you travel on holiday. A long trip around the world will greatly increase your carbon footprint. So, try a green holiday. Travel in large groups and make responsible environmental choices that result in less waste.

Getting it Wrong

Sport utility vehicles (SUVs) are very popular, especially in the United States. Many people like them because they're big and powerful, but they are not very eco-friendly. The low mileage and high petrol consumption means an SUV gets half the mileage per gallon and emits 45 percent more air pollution than the average car.

Older and poorly maintained cars have higher carbon emissions than newer, well-maintained cars. Air pollution associated with higher carbon dioxide levels causes around 22,000 deaths each year.

↓ *Jet travel increases carbon footprints. Each trip uses hundreds of gallons of fuel and emits tons of carbon dioxide.*

Changing your travel choices

Our individual travel choices have a significant impact on the planet. The average person emits almost 100 pounds of carbon dioxide each day – much of it from car and plane travel. If every person took action to reduce his or her travel footprint by even a little, we could drastically cut down on greenhouse gas emissions and keep our air cleaner.

REDUCING YOUR TRAVEL FOOTPRINT

There are many simple things the world's drivers and travellers can do to reduce their impact on the climate. You can also make choices as a family to help reduce your travel footprint.

G Taking public transport

If you don't already, consider taking public transport to school. Many cities have public transport systems that are easy to use. These systems include underground trains, buses, trams, and trains. In many cities, it is possible to live without a car. To travel longer distances, take a train or bus.

G Carpool

Carpooling – or sharing a lift – is an easy way to reduce the number of cars on the road. If you have classmates who live nearby, talk to your parents or a guardian about setting up a carpool. Survey your neighbours to find out how many cars people in their household drive each day. Find out how many people are in each car and where they go. If you discover that people in your local area are driving separately to the same places or pass by the same places on the way, introduce them to one another so they can carpool instead.

G Walk or ride a bike

Depending on where you live, find ways to walk or ride your bike to school, on errands, or to friends' homes. Both are fun activities that can help you stay healthy as well.

Getting it Right

The European Union proposes that car manufacturers should cut the average emissions from cars to 120g of CO_2 per kilometre by 2012. The UK had already cut tailpipe emissions by 13 percent since 1997, to an average of 164.9g/km in 2007. Each vehicle made in the UK requires half the energy to produce than it did just five years ago, saving an estimated 700,000 tonnes of CO_2 each year.

TIP

Remind your parent or guardian to keep the car engine tuned up. Clean, well-tuned engines run more efficiently and emit less pollution. Be sure the tyres are properly inflated as well. This can help you use less fuel!

Talk to your family about changing to an electric car or a hybrid. Hybrids run on two sources of energy: a regular gas engine and a battery-powered motor. At high speeds, the gas engine powers the car and also charges the battery, which then powers the car at lower speeds. Both hybrids and electric cars can reduce emissions. Some cities even have electric or natural gas-powered buses!

A GREEN FUTURE FOR TRAVEL

There are lots of things you and your family can do to reduce your travel emissions. But there are also many new and exciting alternatives being developed to help you further reduce your travel footprint in the future.

Critical Mass is a worldwide movement designed to increase awareness about biking as a healthy, eco-friendly means of transportation. In cities around the world, Critical Mass cyclists have taken to the street in large groups to show their support for biking. The first ride took place in San Francisco in 1992, and events continue to take place once a month in cities around the world. Many of these events attract thousands of cyclists!

G Eco-tourism

Where you go and how you get there determines your holiday's ecological footprint. Eco-tourism is a responsible way to travel that doesn't harm nature or local communities.

Eco-tourism could involve taking a bike or joining a walking tour of a city instead of touring by bus. It can also mean staying in green hotels. Many hotels around the world are reducing their ecological footprint by restricting water use, using energy from sustainable sources, and serving organic foods in their restaurants. Resorts called **eco-lodges**, often located in beautiful natural areas, take

TIP

Reduce your travel miles by looking at cool places to go to nearer home. You'll be surprised what's on offer without needing to travel from country to country. Or you could look into eco-tourism.

this green idea a step further. Eco-tourism lessens the environmental impact of travel and builds environmental awareness.

G Carbon offsets

What if you don't want to give up on travel? Several innovative companies sell **"carbon credits"** that allow consumers and corporations to offset their travel-related emissions. When you buy carbon credits, you pay a company to invest in renewable energy, plant trees, or do something positive for the environment to offset the fossil fuel emissions from your trip.

There is disagreement, however, about how environmentally sound these carbon-offset programmes are. People who support the programmes say that emissions are inevitable, and offsets help reduce the total level of emissions. They can also raise awareness about the need to find alternatives to fossil fuel.

Opponents of carbon credits say that these programmes don't work the way they are supposed to. There are no organisations to oversee the companies selling these credits, so there is no guarantee they are doing what they claim they are. What do you think?

Maybe the best way to reduce your carbon footprint is to stay close to home or choose eco-tourism!

The Problem Of Waste

Have you ever thought about what happens after you throw something away? Where does it go? Does it simply disappear? If only it were that easy! Most of our waste goes into a rubbish dump or landfill, where it slowly biodegrades.

DID YOU KNOW?

Up to 60 percent of the rubbish that ends up being buried at a landfill could be recycled.
As much as 50 percent of the rubbish in an average bin could be composted.

TONS OF RUBBISH

In more economically developed countries, such as the United Kingdom and the United States, each person disposes of more than 450 kilos of rubbish each year. Do you know what percentage of our waste is not biodegradable? More than three quarters of that waste ends up in **landfills**.

Landfills are a major contributor to global warming. As rubbish decomposes in the landfill, it releases greenhouse gases, such as methane. Other methods of waste disposal, such as incineration (burning), also cause problems. Burning certain wastes, such as plastics, releases hazardous gases into the environment. **Toxic waste** disposal presents another big challenge. Even household items, such as batteries, motor oil, and paint, contain poisons that can seep into the ground and contaminate soil and water. As Earth's population continues to rise, waste disposal challenges will only increase.

Eventually we will run out of unused space for new landfills. Then what will we do? We must reduce the amount of rubbish we generate and find better and cleaner ways to dispose of the remaining waste.

How much does your family throw away? Collect a day's worth of your household rubbish and weigh it. Multiply the weight by 365 for an estimate of your family's annual waste. Now think about how much rubbish you will throw away in your lifetime!

Getting it Right

Plastic bags – like the ones you get at most shops – take at least 500 years to break down in a landfill. When they do, they release harmful components into the atmosphere. They also end up as discarded rubbish in the sea and are responsible for the deaths of hundreds and thousands of seabirds and other marine wildlife. In 2007, the small town of Modbury in Devon was the first place in Britain to outlaw the plastic bag. Every trader in the town agreed to encourage shoppers to buy reusable bags. It is now hoped that the 13 billion plastic bags used every year will be reduced. In 2007, Gordon Brown, announced that he would like to "eliminate" single-use plastic bags from Britain.

275,000 tons of plastic are used each year in the UK. That's around 15 million bottles a day!

TIPS FOR REDUCING HOUSEHOLD WASTE

Many people have heard of the "three Rs": reduce, reuse, and recycle. This phrase is a useful way to remember how to address the problem of waste. For more specific ideas, read the following tips and think about how to incorporate them into your daily routine.

Electronic waste, or e-waste, is a growing problem in today's high-tech world. Most e-waste contains over one thousand chemicals, many of which are toxic – this can create serious environmental and health hazards. Computers are especially toxic. In the UK more than a million tons of e-waste such as old computer monitors and discarded mobile phones are thrown away each year. Find a place near your home to recycle electronic waste. Or resist buying new items when the old ones work perfectly well.

ⓖ Reduce packaging

Buy in bulk and avoid items with excess packaging. Choose products in returnable or reusable containers and refill from large, bulk containers.

ⓖ Use reusable shopping bags

Get rid of the plastic bags in your house. But don't just throw them away. Some supermarkets will give you credit for each bag brought in. You can use them to dispose of pet waste, line rubbish bins, or reuse them as shopping bags. When all your plastic bags are gone, don't take any more! Get in to the habit of taking reusable bags to the shops. If a cashier offers a plastic bag, say "No, thank you" and use your reusable one instead.

ⓖ Repair existing appliances

Before you throw away that music player, see if it can be repaired! That way you won't have to buy a new one – or throw your old one in a landfill.

ⓖ Carry a reusable water bottle

Don't buy water bottles – they are wasteful, even if you recycle them. Buy a stainless steel or other reusable bottle to fill with tap water. Decorate with stickers and take everywhere you go!

G Stop junk mail

Junk mail is unwanted mail sent to your home – catalogues, advertisements, takeaway menus. Many countries offer a service that allows you to opt out of direct mail advertising (see page 52 for details). This saves tons of paper from the landfill each year.

G Buy used goods

Many products are available used or refurbished – clothes, books, electronics, and other household goods. Search used bookstores for great reads and bring your outgrown or unwanted clothing to the charity shop. You may even pick up some bargains while you're there! Donating to a charity shop also helps people in need.

G Buy recycled goods

Recycled goods are made from waste, use fewer resources, and offer a more sustainable option. From school supplies to toilet paper, many recycled options are available.

G Reuse

Reusing items, such as shopping bags, boxes, and aluminium foil, reduces the amount you throw in the bin. This can also save money. Use disposable items, such as paper towels, sparingly – use a reusable cloth to clean surfaces instead.

Getting it Right

Make a list of the recycling centres in your area and find out what they recycle. Some centres recycle almost every type of household material, while others only recycle paper and aluminium cans. Create flyers about recycling – on reused or recycled paper, of course – and post them in your neighbour's postboxes.

G Reuse paper

Use the back of copies or printouts that you no longer need as scrap paper. Wrap birthday and other gifts in newspaper rather than using wrapping paper. And remember that in the UK well over 2 million tonnes of rubbish is produced by the Christmas season alone.

G Recycle

Recycling items, such as newspapers, glass, aluminium cans, and plastic bottles, requires less energy than producing new items from raw materials.

Other sources of waste

Schools contribute a lot of waste. Think of all the announcements, forms, and of course, homework you go through in a single day!

Suggest ways your school can reduce waste, such as reusing paper that has only been used on one side. Create a place in your classroom for students and teachers to stack reusable paper. Your class can use that paper for notes or to print documents from the computer. You can even make scrap pads out of that single-sided paper by stapling sheets together.

Compost

Creating your own **compost** bin is a great way to recycle food scraps and garden trimmings. Home composting can keep nearly half of our household waste out of the landfill. You might be surprised to learn how many things can be composted – fruit and

TIP

Before starting a new school year, determine which of your school supplies can be reused or recycled. Notebooks, folders, and binders can all be reused. Reuse or recycle leftover papers and share your used books with younger students.

vegetable scraps, coffee grounds, leaves, grass clippings, weeds, garden debris, and non-recyclable paper products (such as paper towels, napkins, plates, coffee filters, and tea bags). You will need to stir-up your compost to aerate it and help the matter break down. Compost is a great fertiliser for your garden.

Getting it Right

In the United Kingdom, the company WRAP (Waste & Resources Action Programme) works with businesses and consumers to find ways to minimise their use of materials and find more ways to recycle. WRAP's "Recycle Now" campaign spreads the recycling message by television and newspaper advertisements. Its Recycle Now website (see page 52) provides information to help consumers recycle more items. WRAP's goal is to achieve 40 percent recycling rates in the United Kingdom by 2010.

Day 0

Day 12

Day 33

Day 45

Bioplastics are biodegradable containers made from plant products such as corn and wheat. These break down much faster than conventional plastics and release no harmful toxins into the environment. High-quality containers and utensils made from corn can be composted and break down completely in as little as 45 days. If your school uses disposable utensils, ask them to consider making the switch to bioplastics.

WILDLIFE CONSERVATION

Human activity has caused the extinction of thousands of plant and animal species. One reason for this rapid species destruction is overdevelopment. This occurs when people use natural resources in a non-sustainable way.

HUMAN INVASION

Much of Earth's **wilderness** areas are being developed for human use, which destroys precious animal habitats. Activities such as logging, mining, fishing, ranching, farming, and construction all contribute to habitat destruction.

Another problem is **urbanisation**, or the spread of human development into natural habitats. As populations spread out farther and farther from dense city centres, trees are cut down and fields destroyed to create space for more houses. Fast-growing, metropolitan areas rapidly consume land that is essential to the survival of many species. Continuing overdevelopment all over the world is predicted to completely destroy some essential wildlife habitats in the next 20 years.

Widespread **overfishing** has greatly reduced the world's fish populations. In the last 50 years, the world's appetite for seafood has outpaced the ability of fish populations to replenish themselves. Industrial fishing operations have exploited 52 percent of the world's fisheries, while 24 percent are overexploited, depleted, or recovering from collapse.

Getting it Right

In 1986 the Earth Island Institute organised a boycott of canned tuna to urge companies to use safer tuna nets. At the time, many dolphins were becoming trapped in tuna nets and dying. In 1990 many of the world's biggest tuna corporations agreed to stop selling tuna caught in unsafe nets. However, there are still issues surrounding tuna fishing as many tuna stock are over-exploited. Greenpeace recommends that you only buy line-caught, skipjack tuna.

Save the rainforests

Rainforests are a crucial part of Earth's delicate ecosystem. The Amazon rainforest accounts for more than half of the world's remaining rainforest area. More than one-third of the world's species call this warm, moist area home. But the Amazon rainforest is in danger. Vast areas of trees are being cut down so the land may be used for ranching and agriculture. **Deforestation** destroys habitats and puts many species at risk of extinction.

Rainforests also fulfill an important environmental function; they act as **carbon sinks**. Trees, plants, and soil have a natural ability to remove carbon dioxide from the atmosphere, so they actually clean the air and reduce greenhouse gases. In a way, they are Earth's natural self-cleaning mechanism! This shows the important role wilderness areas play in fighting climate change. We must act fast to stop rainforest destruction and preserve the ecological balance of these important areas.

↓ *Deforestation, as shown here in the Amazon rainforest of Brazil, destroys habitats for endangered species that live there. It also reduces the biodiversity of the entire planet!*

WHAT YOU CAN DO

Because human activity has such a great impact on the Earth's ecosystems, altering our daily habits can make a big difference in how our lifestyle affects the environment.

Ⓖ Use your consumer power

Purchase sustainably harvested products to avoid destroying habitats.

Ⓖ Adopt an animal

What's your favourite wild animal? Many organisations such as the World Wide Fund for Nature (WWF) have programmes where you can adopt an animal by giving money towards protecting its habitat.

Ⓖ Organise a park or beach cleanup

Is there a park in your area? Do you live near the ocean, a lake, or a river? With help from a parent, guardian, or teacher, organise a group of friends and classmates to pick up litter in one of these areas.

Ⓖ Encourage green growth

Feed the birds by hanging bird feeders or leaving out seeds. Plant trees, flowers, and shrubs to encourage bees and butterflies to visit your garden.

Ⓖ Don't wear animal products

Fur and leather are both animal products that involve the killing of animals for their skin. Avoid clothing and shoes made from the skin of exotic species, many of which are endangered.

Ⓖ Avoid animal testing

Check to see if your personal care products are tested on animals. Products that don't test on animals often state this on the label, for example: "cruelty free" – choose these products instead.

DID YOU KNOW?

Many of the products we use on our bodies are tested for safety before we can buy and use them. One way of testing the products is by using animals. Testers see if the products make the animals sick or give them skin irritations. Millions of animals are used to test products every year.

Speak out in favour of preserving green spaces and woodland areas in your neighbourhood. It is important to make your voice heard! Being able to communicate effectively will help you make a difference in your community. Write letters to your neighbours about the importance of conserving wildlife habitat in your area. Send letters to newspapers about the need to preserve nature. Find your local government representatives and write to them – ask them to take action!

G Keep your garden green

There are many things you can do to make your garden more wildlife friendly. Don't keep your garden too tidy! Leave seed heads for the birds in winter months. Avoid using toxic chemicals such as pesticides or chemical fertilisers. Find environmentally friendly methods of pest control. Use vinegar or other harmless substances, or use physical controls such as sticky barriers to prevent ants and other insects from feeding on garden plants. Copper tape can also be used to block access to snails and slugs. Preserve the natural balance of your garden by using organic fertiliser!

Local communities can make a big difference by cleaning up pollution that is dumped in nearby streams or fields. This can help improve the health and beauty of your local environment!

A Sustainable Lifestyle

Going green is a way of life. The choices you make every day have a direct effect on Earth's environment. Be aware that your choices can influence those of others.

Inspiring Changes

Reduce your environmental impact – starting right now! Get into the habit of doing things differently and you'll find changes easier to follow.

Work with your family to find ways of reducing your household footprint. Remember: you have power as a consumer. The things you buy, foods you eat, and energy you use all have an impact on Earth's delicate ecosystem. Being aware of your environmental footprint helps you understand the consequences of your choices.

You can make a difference on a global level by acting in your local community. Don't underestimate the power of the individual to change the world!

DID YOU KNOW?

In April and November of 2007, Step It Up, a group concerned with climate change, organised rallies in hundreds of U.S. cities. The purpose of these gatherings was to raise awareness of climate change and push the U.S. government to reduce carbon dioxide emissions. Hundreds of politicians and community leaders attended local events.

20 ways to reduce your carbon footprint			
Energy	Turn off lights and appliances.	Air dry your clothes.	Adjust your thermostat.	Switch to fluorescent bulbs.
Travel	Bike or walk.	Carpool.	Take public transport.	Take holidays nearer home.
Waste	Buy less packaging.	Recycle.	Buy used and renewable goods.	Compost.
Food	Buy local.	Buy organic.	Buy less processed food.	Eat more vegetarian meals.
Water	Turn off the tap.	Choose cold water.	Buy less bottled water.	Don't dump rubbish down the drain.

Today's students are tomorrow's leaders

Hopefully after reading this book you are more aware of the problems facing our environment – and the solutions. Talk to your parents, your friends, your teachers, and your neighbours about things every person on this planet can do to GET GREEN!

Global warming (climate change) is perhaps the biggest issue facing the world today. Citizens like you can become involved and influence the way that governments address this problem that affects us all!

Getting it Right

Kids FACE (Kids For A Clean Environment) is one of the world's largest youth environmental organisations. It has more than 2,000 club chapters in 15 countries and more than 300,000 individual members. Kids FACE provides information on environmental issues to encourage young people to take action.

QUIZ RESULTS

HOW GREEN ARE YOU?
For page 9

If you answered mostly:

a) you have good green awareness. Learn new ways to get green with this book. Use these ideas to help your family and friends get green. Keep up the good work!

b) you are on your way to green living. This book can help you discover more ways to make your lifestyle greener and bring your family and friends along with you.

c) this is the book for you! As you read, be sure to pay attention to ways you can develop a greener lifestyle. You can play an important role in helping your friends and family get green, too!

WHAT'S YOUR FOOD FOOTPRINT?
For page 17

If you answered mostly:

a) you have a small eco-footprint. Your family makes green food choices. Keep it up and ask your friends about their footprint.

b) you are on your way to a green diet. Go to the supermarket with a parent or guardian and look for green food choices you can make.

c) look for delicious ways to green your diet. Find a vegetarian, local, or organic restaurant in your neighbourhood where your family can get some good ideas.

HOW ENERGY SMART ARE YOU?
For page 25

1) False.
2) Ten times.
3) True.
4) True.

②⓪ THINGS TO REMEMBER

1 Get in the habit of turning off lights when you leave a room. This reduces energy consumption and saves money.

2 Stop throwing away plastic water bottles. Purchase a reusable bottle and fill it from water fountains throughout the day.

3 Reduce the amount of packaging you buy. Search for produce that is not already packaged and avoid buying individually packaged snacks.

4 Recycle! See how much you can reduce the waste you throw away. Learn more about your community's recycling programme and encourage your family and friends to buy recycled products.

5 Compost your waste. If you are gardening, a personal compost bin provides free fertiliser for your plants.

6 Turn off the water when brushing your teeth to reduce water consumption.

7 Take your own shopping bag to the shops.

8 Use an old towel or cloth to clean up spills, instead of paper towels.

9 Put on a jumper instead of turning up the heat to help you stay warm without consuming energy.

10 Turn on a fan instead of the air conditioner.

11 Buy organic food. See what options exist in your supermarket.

12 Buy local food. This reduces the energy needed to transport food all around the world.

13 Find alternative ways to get to school – bike or walk.

14 Carpool or combine trips to cut down on driving.

15 Eat less meat. Vegetarian meals use less energy to produce and are often healthier for you.

16 Find air leaks in your house. Insulation will help you use less energy to climate control your house.

17 Reuse paper – write on both sides and reuse sheets for scrap paper.

18 Make smart consumer choices. Companies will respond to what we buy, so be a green customer.

19 If you have a suggestion about ways to green your area, write to your political representative and let them know!

20 Spread the word! Tell your friends and community! Share ideas learned in this book and use your imagination. What are other ways you can GET GREEN?

Further Information

Websites

http://www.urbanext.uiuc.edu/worms/
Great composting advice from Herman the worm.

http://www.ase.org/uploaded_files/educatorlessonplans/audit.pdf
Ways to audit your energy base.

http://www.eia.doe.gov/kids/energyfacts/sources/whatsenergy.html
Energy facts from the U.S. Department of Energy.

http://www.myfootprint.org
Find out your ecological footprint.

http://www.nrdc.org/greensquad/
Join the Green Squad.

http://www.davidsuzuki.org/kids/
Ten challenges for staying green.

http://www.mpsonline.org.uk
Stop junk mail.

http://www.kidsface.org
Join other green kids.

http://www.gardenorganic.org.uk/schools_organic_network
Learn about gardening.

http://www.uni.edu/earth/EECP/elem/mod2_math.html
Measure your household energy usage.

http://www.recyclenow.com
Check out WRAP's site for tips, facts, and information.

BOOKS/GUIDES

Kids Container Gardening: Year-Round Projects for Inside and Out, Bruce Curtis and Cindy Krezel (Ball Publishing, 2005).

Planet Under Pressure: Climate Change, Mike Unwin (Raintree, 2007).

Recycle!: A Handbook for Kids, Gail Gibbons (Little, Brown Young Readers, 1996).

Reduce, Reuse, Recyle! An Easy Household Guide, Nicky Scott (Green Books, 2004).

The Little Book of Green Living, Mark Hegarty (Nightingale Press, 2007).

This Is My Planet: The Kids' Guide to Global Warming, Jan Thornhill (Maple Tree Press, 2007).

You Can Save The Planet, Jacquie Wines (Buster Books, 2007).

You Can Save The Planet, Rich Hough (A&C Black, 2007).

50 Simple Things You Can do to Save the Earth: Completely New and Updated for the 21st Century, Jesse Javna, John Javna and Sophie Javna (Hyperion, 2008).

GLOSSARY

agricultural runoff water from industrial farms that carries chemicals and animal waste and threatens ecosystems

alternative energy energy derived from renewable resources, such as solar, hydropower, and wind energy

biodegradable capable of decomposing (breaking down) rapidly under natural conditions

biodiesel fuel produced from renewable biological resources, such as plant matter, vegetable oil, or treated waste

biodiversity number and variety of living organisms that create an ecological balance necessary for healthy ecosystems

boycott refuse to have any part of, or decide not to buy something, usually as a form of protest

carbon credit/carbon offset way individuals, companies, and governments pay for their carbon emissions

carbon sink area of vegetation, such as rainforests, that removes carbon from the atmosphere through the process of photosynthesis

climate change changes in weather patterns due to rising global temperatures as a result of natural temperature variation and human activity

compact fluorescent light bulb type of bulb that uses less energy and has a longer life than incandescent bulbs

compost pile of organic matter that decomposes to form nutrients that feed plants

conserve save a natural resource, such as water, through wise use

deforestation cutting down trees in a very large area

ecological footprint area of land needed to support an individual, family, or population

ecosystem complex system of organisms and their environment that functions as a single unit

emission release of greenhouse gas into the atmosphere

fair trade better trading conditions that protect the rights of producers and their communities, often those located in the Third World

food mile distance food travels from its place of production to the consumer, or from farm to table

fossil fuel fuel formed from decayed plants and animals, such as oil and coal

Gaia hypothesis the idea that Earth is a living system

global warming increasing global temperatures caused by climate change as a result of natural temperature variation and human activity

grey water household wastewater from non-toilet sources that can be used for irrigation

greenhouse gas gas that traps the Sun's energy and causes warming in the atmosphere

hypothesis proposal intended to explain certain facts or ideas

incandescent emitting light by being heated

industrial agriculture large-scale farms that grow one or two crops and take a heavy toll on the environment

landfill place where refuse is buried.

natural resource something that occurs in nature that has value to humans, such as timber, fresh water, or mineral deposits

non-renewable energy source of energy that cannot be replenished quickly, such as oil

ore mineral that contains metal that is valuable enough to be mined

organic grown or prepared without the use of chemicals or pesticides

overfishing practice of harvesting the ocean's wildlife beyond levels that can sustain the population

pesticides chemical used to kill pests, especially insects

renewable energy energy obtained from sources that are unlimited or quickly replenished

sustainable meeting the needs of the present without compromising future needs

toxic waste waste that poses a significant hazard to the environment or human health

turbine device that converts the flow of air or water into electricity

urbanisation human development of wild land into cities or residential areas

vegetarian eating a plant-based diet (no meat)

wilderness land that is wild or untouched by humans

Index